SOMETHING HAPPENED IN NORMAL TOWN

A COLLECTION OF POEMS BY

CHRIS SHAW

cjmcshaw@outlook.com

All illustrations are edited from my private photographs.

Independently published
ISBN: 9798865208792

For Joe and Alex, my family, the women I loved and the friends who believed in me.

Contents

The Moving Finger writes; and, having writ,
Moves on: nor all thy Piety nor Wit
Shall lure it back to cancel half a Line,
Nor all thy Tears wash out a Word of it.

Omar Khayyám[1]

[1] from Edward Fitzgerald's English translation: The Rubáiyát of Omar Khayyám, first published 1859.

Prologue

I always think that any old fool can write poetry, and I should know. I am that fool. It might not be to the level of the historical and renowned poets; it may not be studiously constructed. It may not be ground-breaking, it may be corny and lame, predictable and simple but when it flows from mind, soul or heart to page it is a most rewarding, if sometimes frustrating pursuit.

Poetry can record a moment in time, deep emotions, silly thoughts or heartfelt views and philosophies. Poetry can be expressive and cathartic, better out than in.

I never felt that I had the credentials be a proper poet, but I can have a go.

Maybe I disrespect my own intellect by labelling myself as a fool? Although memory and vocabulary are not and never have been my greatest strengths, I love the melody of words, I can read and write, and I know my way around a dictionary and thesaurus.

I was educated at a Grammar School but felt like an imposter. My education was state funded, but I was surrounded by fee payers, entitled kids, and even amongst those who received the same free education as me, many seemed to be smarter, potentially brilliant academic achievers. I was out of my depth. My peers could outsmart me and outperform me in the classroom.

As a pupil destined to be mid-table in most subjects, including English Literature, poetry was the thing that inspired me. Poets spoke to me in a way that novelists and playwrights never got close to.

Poems, on the whole have a beautiful brevity and rhythm, they are able to put complexity into an easy-to-read concise format. Poetry defines moments, generations and situations throughout history. A relatable, efficient form of expression to entertain, amuse, absorb or explain.

I rebelled against my educational circumstance rather than embracing it. For a misunderstood, out of step teenager, Larkin, Auden, Sassoon et al, felt like kindred spirits. They helped me to understand and make sense of a world into which I didn't feel that I fitted.

Away from school my environment was full of poetry. Acclaimed contemporary poets such as John Cooper Clarke and Benjamin Zephaniah blended with the great lyricists of music, including my teenage heroes, John Lennon and Paul Weller. Poems even appeared in the world of comedy with story tellers such as Spike Milligan, Mike Harding and Max Boyce.

My sister, Susan, and one of my best mates, David, wrote poetry much better than I could. They seemed far more literate than me, and were able to create sophisticated works, which were more profound and cerebral than my early writing attempts.

My Mum volunteered to teach English to adults who had literacy difficulties, she used poetry as a part of her curriculum. Mum can still spout lines from classic poems as pearls of wisdom to comment on real-life situations. '*The Moving Finger…*' was always a particular favourite. My Dad also volunteered; he taught school children who struggled with English. One of his most successful and popular methods was to create simple, often amusing rhymes to enable them to understand the complexity of spelling and grammar.

As a young man I aspired to be a rock star and so I began to experiment with verse as I tried to write songs. Most of my earliest attempts are now lost in time. It's probably a blessing. I never did become a rock star, instead I went to work in a normal job in Normal Town. I stopped writing poetry... Life got in the way.

During the nineties I would write occasionally but it was the new millennium and some life difficulties that reignited my passion for rhyme and rhythm.

Since then, I have documented many life experiences, either my own or those of others, via the poetic vehicle. Some were shared amongst family and friends; they seemed to like them. Eventually I created a reputation as some sort of wordsmith and I have been commissioned to write for occasions including birthdays, anniversaries, work events and even funerals. My personalised creations were well received as they offered comfort, amusement and hope.

Always the imposter, I usually love my latest poem, then as time passes, I begin to doubt its validity.

Many an acquaintance has encouraged me to do something with my collection of poems. I did manage to get a couple of things included in low circulation journals and once even appeared on local radio; but living in Normal Town, I had no connections and no idea as to how to get my stuff published.

Eventually I was given some advice and information about self-publishing. So here it is, a collection of poems spanning years and decades. Written by me, an imposter, a normal bloke from Normal Town.

NORMAL TOWN

Come and wander the imaginary streets of Normal Town and meet some of the real people who live there...

Something Happened in Normal Town

Nothing happened in Normal Town
So I slipped back under my eiderdown,
I realised the world was spinning round
And it was not for me.

Nothing happened on Average Street
So I buried my head under my sheet.
I realised that budgies had bacon feet
Or so it seemed to me.

On Typical Road there was no news
So I turned my alarm clock onto snooze
And realised that I had to give up the booze
Before it gave up me.

And while I slept...

At closing time on Regular Lane last night
A drunken youth got into a fight,
He was hit with a bottle but they saved his sight
At the infirmary.

The old lady who lives over the back
Had a sudden heart attack,
She was taken away by the men in black,
To the cemetery.

The sad spinster whose dad had the stroke,
Finally copped off with that shy bloke.
Mind you,
She had to get him pissed on vodka and Coke
Before he would agree.

At 4, Usual Terrace, the perfect mother
Decided it was time to take a lover.
It just happened to be her husbands' brother,
Keep it in the family.

Specky-four-eyes with no money
Was picked up in a limo by a Playboy bunny.
She flew away with him to somewhere sunny,
He'd won the lottery.

In Bog Standard Gardens the local vet
Started a business on the internet.
He's just bought himself a private jet,
Some people just get lucky.

"WAKE UP! You lazy git, come round!"

"GET UP! You lazy shit, come down!"

Something happened in Normal Town
But it didn't happen to me.

House Minder

My mother-in-law often visits my house.
She has a tendency to tidy.
When I come home,
Nothing is where it should be.

She has a tendency to iron.
So when I come back,
Most of my things are flat.

I come home for quiet and peace,
But I can't find them because she's tidied them away,
And there is a distinct crease
In each leg of my scruffy jeans.

I know when my mother-in-law has been to town
Because the contents of my kitchen
Have been swapped around.

I look in the cupboard for my brown sauce,
It's not there, of course.
It is in the fridge...
Ironed!

The Sweeper

What is this time?

Why am I overtaken by this thing that can't be done?

It must be done!

Sweep it under the carpet.
The brush is in my hands,
but there is no carpet in this room,
there is no carpet at this house,
there is no carpet in this life.

Move it around on hard floors,
propel it into corners
unlikely to be revisited.

If by chance rediscovered one day,
I will pick up my brush again.
Perpetual sweeping.

Some of it gets lost in bristles
which in turn pick up new, unrelated dust.
Until one day the thing being swept
won't be that thing at all,
just the dust picked up by all the sweeping.

What was it anyway?

Now spread so thin
that it no longer exists,
but still represented in my mind by the dust.

And so I sweep!

I used to weep and sweep
but now I weep no more.

I wept so much, I swept so much,
I lost what I was weeping for,

I lost what I was sweeping for

but still I sweep.

Old Man

Half a sandwich short of a picnic,
He wanders around the grounds.
Some people call him nitwit but
He never makes a sound.

He is the human scarecrow
But if you knew what he knows,
You might not give him stick,
Might not judge so quick.

He was once a soldier
Who fought in faraway lands,
He was once a surfer
On Australian golden sands,
He once held a princess
But had her taken from his hands.

He was once a policeman
Who wore his badge with pride,
He was once a fisherman
Who sailed the morning tide,
He was always an honest man
Who never tried to hide.

Thicky, stinky no-mates
Shout naughty girls and boys.
He just smiles as insults fly
And never makes a noise.

He is the human scarecrow
But if you knew what he knows,
You might not take the mick,
Might not call him thick.

He was once a chef
Who prepared many fantastic feasts,
He was once an animal keeper
Who tamed the wildest beasts,
He once sought inner harmony
As he travelled the mystic east.

He was once a racing driver
Who drove at breakneck speed,
He once built a business empire
But felt consumed by greed,
He was always a generous man
Who gave to those in need.

Scruffy, scabby sad man,
Around the grounds he walks.
Stared at by every passer-by,
He never stops and talks.

He is the human scarecrow
But if you knew what he knows,
You might feel a little sick
That you call him a lunatic.

He was once a master craftsman
Who created with skilled hands,
He was once a pilgrim
Searching for the Promised Land,

He was a musician
Who toured the world with his rocking band.

He was once a farmer
Who kept our green fields green,
He was once the husband
Of a well-known beauty queen,
He was once the greatest dad
The world has ever seen.

Horrible ugly bag man,
Spanner short of a toolbox.
Beard-o-weirdo hag man
Odd eyes, odd hair, odd socks.

Now he is just an old man,
A left out in the cold man,
Down the river he's been sold man.

Who knows how long he'll live now?
He may not last the year,
But he's done more than you'll ever do
In the time that he's spent here.

Respect to the human scarecrow,
Paid up member of the human scare crew
And if you know half of what he knows
You'll realise one day he'll be you!

Worldly Words

I like using words melodically
Although sometimes I admit, ironically
And even dare I say, sardonically.

But I like words because
They're the only conduit
To express my thoughts.

Thoughts that however insignificant to the world,
Still mean the world to me.

For Christopher

Day upon day the Sun rises and the sun sets
And the same sun is seen by generation upon
generation.

Night upon night the stars shimmer in distant skies
And the night sky remains unchanged millennium upon
millennium.

Longevity, predictability, perceived normality,
And all the world accepts that that is how it is.

But for the few who are in the right place
At the right time,
The extraordinary happens in the night sky,
A bright shooting star traverses the heavens,
Its brightness and its brevity make it remarkable.

Those who see it will remember it forever
And for a brief moment the world is a better place.
They will tell of their magical experience
And feel privileged that they were chosen to share it.

Gibberish

Gibberish, gibberish, I talk gibberish.
Not Yiddish or Piggish or English!

I talk balderdash,
Higgledy-piggledy nonsense
And trash.

Am I a man or a mouse-mat?

Literary Headcase

Returning to the scene of the crime,
With the benefit of hindsight and time,
It seems that what happened here,
Was upon reflection, onomatopoeia!

"FFMMUMPH!"
I said, as you kicked me in the head.

"OUCHAYAOOH!"
Said I, as you poked me in the eye.

"OFFALLAUMPH!"
I cried, as you punched me in the guts.

"ARRARARAOOHMMAH!"
A swift kick in the nuts.

Being beaten up by you
Created some lovely new words.
We could have put them in a dictionary
If anyone had heard.

They're indelibly marked on my memory
So I've written them down above,
Along with the tattoos on your fists
Which one hit me **HATE** or **LOVE**?

I do hope it was the latter
As that would make me chuckle,
To be completely splattered
By your loving knuckle.

So here's an ironic parting thought,
I bet you never knew
That it was literary inspiration
To be beaten up by you.

To think that people call you a thug,
Neanderthal and witless,
When you can make such lovely words
By beating someone shitless.

Misery

The slate is grey and so are you.

It makes me wonder what life threw
To make you feel so blue.

When you smile you look alright
But you keep on frowning and invite...

No sunshine,
No fun,
No light,

Just Misery!

Geeky Gangster

What do you know about my trade?
It's a mystery that will never be solved.
You rely on my skills, it's how I get paid
And that's how my career has evolved.

I write the code upon which you rely,
I supply you with the technical solution,
I weave a web of such complexity
That it becomes an essential contribution.

Like the old map makers of the A-to-Z books,
I fill my work with my trademark eccentricity.
So smart that if anyone clever enough ever
looks,
They won't understand its complexity.

It will cost many years and plenty of cash
For an outsider to decode my methodology.
I've created a safe place, I've done my maths
And I know that you can't live without me.

Sit down at my virtual card table and play,
The deck is stacked, I'm always the winner.
My unfathomable logic will win the day.
I'm a grand master and you're a beginner.

So challenge and criticise me, I can resist,
I'm a card trick magician, a nerdy prankster.
I've created a world in which only I can exist.
You've been fooled by the Geeky Gangster.

Strange Kat Strut

One kool kat...

Strutting down the alley in his worn-out spats,
Trying to get a tune out of an old fake Strat,
Fine dining on junk that'll make him fat.

Whispering his lyrics about his worn-out day,
Dreaming of the person that can make him stray,
Needing the religion that can make him pray,
Dancing to the rhythmic beat of yesterday.

One kool dude...

Living on a diet of liquid food,
Trying to break old bonds without appearing rude,
Wanting to go and do it but not feeling in the mood.

Fumbling with fashion just to find some style,
Picking up the phone but not being able to dial,
Finding opportunities but running a mile,
Crying on the inside while the outside tries to smile.

One kool man...

Running down an alley where he never should have ran,
Aiming to survive because he knows that he can,
Lying in the shade and still expecting a tan.

Losing his identity then trying to get it back,
Seeking the bravery that he'll always lack,
Meandering and swaying down his well-worn track,
Waiting for his next anxiety attack.

That old man river, he's a taker not a giver,
He's a lover not a fighter,
He's a wronger not a righter,
He can't win but still he'll try to,
He won't win but thinks he might do.

One kool kat...

Still believes and there's nothing wrong with that.
One day the fashion might be worn out spats
And the tunes the lady sings to
Might be played on old fake Strats.

FAMILY

Home is where the heart is in Normal Town, come and meet some of my family...

Boys

I love my sons, I love my sons,
My pride and joy the only ones
Who matter more to me
Than anything that could ever be,
Who matter more to me
Than they can ever know,
More than my words and deeds can ever show.

They teach me things that can't be taught,
They think the things I never thought.
They live in worlds I cannot share,
I've no intention of going there.
There is no invitation and I've no inclination,
I'm happy here watching on,
Waiting for news of what they've done.

Feeling proud and laughing out loud
Or crying inside when things go bad
And trying to hide it just like a dad.
Here with my ear to the ground,
Waiting for a sign or sound, a distant communiqué,
Some scrambled message from far away.
Something to say: “We're Ok!”

Deciphering and decrypting the white noise.

I love my boys, I love my boys.

Daddy Cool

There is nothing sad about my dad,
And I should know,
I've known him since I was a little lad,
He helped me grow
To be a man that sees a laugh
And a hug and a happy smile,
As being the only things in life
That are truly worthwhile.

There is nothing bad about my dad,
In my slightly biased view.
He's the best friend that I've ever had
Upstanding, honest and true.
A totally dependable man
And it's certainly no surprise
When people say there is nothing
About him to despise.

There is nothing cold about my old man,
He's warm and understanding,
The highly respected man that can,
Whilst remaining undemanding.
Never judging, he's ungrudging
And pragmatic
Whilst underneath, deep down at heart,
A secret romantic.

There is nothing weak about my father,
He can tough it out.
When other people might not rather,
A true competitor no doubt.

You can take him on
If that’s your choosing
But it's highly likely that you'll end up losing.

There is nothing stupid about my predecessor,
When facts become obscure
He's smarter than a college professor
And even when unsure
His patient and determined contribution
Will bloody-mindedly find
An inevitable solution.

There is nothing negative about my patriarch,
No reasons to hide.
With a positive charge he lights up the dark,
“Look on the bright side!”
He's amazing and witty
And clever and great
Age and time don’t matter,
He'll always be my best mate.

My Mum’s Catering

A rattling of pans in the kitchen
The smashing of glass in the hall.
There's a shout of mild desperation,
My mum's catering for us all.

There's a weird, disjointed conversation
That gets heard through the living room wall.
The subject’s bizarre but it needs no translation,
My mum's catering for us all.

She flies in through the door like a whippet,
“Are you listening to me when I call?”
Then she unfurls her wisdom snippet by snippet,
My mum's catering for us all.

Back to the kitchen there's smoke and steam,
Plates and dishes big and small.
There's the odd “bloody hell” or an oven burn scream,
My mum's catering for us all.

“Have you set the table? You shape like my arse!”
She'll rattle and cackle and bawl.
She sets the scene for a new English farce,
My mum's catering for us all.

We'll sit down to eat, a bit later than most.
Her mad stories and anecdotes will enthral,
As we throw in one-liners and carve up the roast,
My mum's catering for us all.

Starters, main course and afters
Get punctuated with the tales she'll recall.
Joy and hilarity rise up to the rafters,
My mum's catering for us all.

She clears up the table until nothing remains
Then curls up on the settee in a ball.
Barking her orders for quizzes and games,
My mum's catering for us all.

She’s survived the ordeals of life,
She’s seen war, hard times and the odd brawl,
As a great daughter, mum, granny and wife,
My mum’s catered for us all.

One Forest One Tree

My little boy, my son, my child has turned into an ex-child,
A more mature version of his person soon to be voluntarily exiled.

An exiled ex-child released and unleashed into a new unknown.
Harvested from seeds lovingly, if somewhat haphazardly sewn.
From a tiny sapling in an urban English garden something special keeps on growing
As wonderful new shoots, branches, leaves, flowers and fruits begin showing.

He is a vibrant, wonderful forest contained in a single tree.
A blend of hardiness and fragility, mixed with beauty and variety.
Unlike other less elaborate species, he isn't rooted to the ground,
His unrestrained spirit, mind and body are free to move around.

He is a play of complexity, a gripping novel, an amazing musical interlude,
A building of architectural delight, a dance of joy, a landscape of great magnitude.
If the greatest works of creativity and discovery emanate from the heart,

Then he is a wonderful achievement,
a piece of living art.

He has transformed potential energy into a light
that will shine and brighten
In Japan, where he will gain and pass on wisdom
to enhance and enlighten,
And it makes me proud and happy and though
I may miss him when he's gone,
In the land of the rising Sun there will be
a new and wising son,
my son.

One Forest One Tree (II)

One forest one tree
Sewn and grown in my garden
To the rising Sun

LOVE & SEPARATION

The world needs love and so do the people of Normal Town. Sometimes things don’t quite work out as planned but love will always leave its mark...

Now

Sitting down one afternoon
as day ended and so began
the night,
the time of life.
I thought of you and knew
that I'd never find you again,
that you had gone forever.

But you were there
at the outset,
at the inset.
On the instep,
on the doorstep,
on the floor,
laying by my side.

Rising with the moon,
setting with the sun
being alive when the world begun.
When it ends,
I'm there with you,
being near you,
laying in you.

Let the world stand still for one second.
Let it just be the two of us,
Because now is everything.

Forever Autumn

When the sunshine's gone and my summer is over
And I take a look at my four leaved clover
In the fading light,

Then I'm afraid I might have to agree,
That what I thought was four leaves
May only be three.

And the sunshine good luck
That I hung my hopes upon
Took an autumn down-turn and is almost all gone.

In the fading auburn, autumn light
I may have to decree that
The imagined good fortune sign isn't really for me.

My sunshine mind in the summer season
Gave me a feeling and a reason to be me,
The version of me that I always wanted to be

And whilst we might not always be together,
Thanks to the summer I'll be that man forever.

The Moth

Eyes that shine through darkness, skin that invites
my fingers to caress it so gently and so slowly.

Smile that makes my heart yearn. The touch of lips
still lingers. If only you knew what I was thinking.

Moth to a flame, the feeling impossible to resist!

Downhill on my bicycle to crash into the wall,

I won’t try to stop. Freewheeling.

I know I have brakes, but they elude me...

Danger hot flame, but it glows so brightly!

The remains of those who’ve gone before
lay dormant.

I saw them try to touch the flame but
Fail and flail and burn and fall.

So why then even try? Though try I must!

Moth to a flame, the feeling impossible to resist!

Extinguish please, turn out the light.

Let the darkness return me to dangerless flight.

But you don't even know that it's lit...

Why little moth do you do it?

Is it because you can't reason?

Why little moth did you do it?
You must have had warnings.
You must have been scorched.

Yet still you came back for more.
To now, to this morbid stench,
Smouldering on the floor.

Intellect tells me
That two and two is four.
I understand cause and effect,
I can foresee.

So why little moth do I do it?

Make some room on the floor
Just for me.

New Rainbow

I may not amount to very much,
Not handsome, suave or butch.
I may not be the type of bloke
That everyone needs to know.

But I've lived my life in colour,
Barbie pink to laser blue
And I've seen a whole new rainbow
In the time I've spent with you.

My eyes are not striking,
Not Newman or Bacall
And my assets aren't golden,
In fact, I've got sod all.

But I've lived my life in colour,
Winter white to summer green
And the colours that you show me
Are the best I've ever seen.

So stop for a moment,
Take a new look at every day.
If you only allow the black and white then
Everything turns grey.
Life's too short for monochrome
It's not a wartime Movietone.

If you open up your eyes and open up your soul,
You can know,
Be free to go
Into a whole new rainbow.

There've been times when things I've done
Have lacked finesse and style
But even so in retrospect,
They sometimes make me smile,

Because I've lived my life in colour,
Gravy brown to tikka red
And the flavours that you taste of
Are the best I've ever had.

I'm exploring life in colour,
Every tone and every hue
And I see a whole new rainbow
Every time I look at you.

If you open up your eyes and open up your soul
You can know,
Be free to go
Into a whole new rainbow.

Shake Rattle and Roll

When I kissed you goodbye
At the start of your journey
I always thought you'd be returning home.
Little did I know that the timetable in your mind
Was not the same as mine
And your empathetic smile
Did not reveal the many miles
That we had somehow drifted apart,
Before I watched you walk away.

You didn't say, you never said,
You just walked away and waved
But in your head,
Something was dead,
Something that I thought was living
Something that my soul was still giving
Was lost in the busy rush
And the dizzy push and shove
As you weaved through crowds and took my love...

...Away.

To platform thirteen,
The one that can't be seen.
The one that's hidden in the upper space,
The one where I couldn't see your face
As it blended in with the rat race
And went off to another place,
A place that I will never share;

On your one-way ticket to somewhere...

...Else.

The tracks shake and rattle
As the fast-approaching train rolls in
With a screech of brakes
And takes you away...

...Unseen.

From platform thirteen,

And the platform in the sky empties

With an empty goodbye.

The Day Your Shoes Fell in Love with Me

I was just walking down the street,
Normal boring footwear on my feet,
You were the last person I expected to meet,
The day your shoes fell in love with me.

I would have just looked the other way,
Got on with the rest of my boring day,
But there was something said that words couldn't say,
The day your shoes fell in love with me.

The day your shoes fell in love with me,
The day your shoes fell in love with me,
They showed me things that I should never see,
Made me into something that I could never be.

Walk the walk,
Talk the talk,
Think the think,
Do the do.

It was extraordinary,
The day your shoes fell in love with me.

I was frightened without real fears,
Crying sanctimonious tears,
Missing the point and losing years,
The day your shoes fell in love with me.

I didn't think I had a lot,
And what I did have I'd forgot,
I thought that all that was, was not,

The day your shoes fell in love with me.

The day your shoes fell in love with me,
The day your shoes fell in love with me,
They showed me things that I could never see,
Made me into something that I should never be.

Walk the walk,
Talk the talk,
Think the think,
Do the do.

It was extraordinary,
The day your shoes fell in love with me.

They took me completely by surprise,
I didn't even contemplate their size,
But they made me look up into your eyes,
The day your shoes fell in love with me.

So now I hold my head up high,
Now I no longer need to cry,
You took away the reasons why,
The day your shoes fell in love with me.

The day your shoes fell in love with me,
The day your shoes fell in love with me,
They showed me things that I should never see,
Made me into something that I would never be,

And I thank God, whoever he or she may be,
For the day your shoes fell in love with me.

Nobody Nose

There is something about the way you smell
That seems to cast a spell on me.
It starts off up my nose
And then gets all over my clothes
And God only knows why I like it so much,
That I can't get enough of it.

You might be inclined to think
That I'm saying that you stink, I'm not!
It's just something ever present,
A nasal sensation that's so pleasant
A scent that I adore, that makes me want you more
And I can't get enough of it.

I don't think that it's hormonal,
It certainly isn't anything abnormal,
It's not something manufactured
But it makes me feel enraptured.
It can't be bottled or captured
And I can't get enough of it.

Every time I get a sniff of you,
It makes me happy to be with you.
There is something about my olfaction
That has some weird aromatic reaction,
Which creates an inescapable attraction,
And I can't get enough of it.

So Near Yet So Far

Young lives, young minds in a tiny town.
Close-knit groups of disparate age tread common ground,
Some of whom pass by in hard to see futures
When you can't look the present in the eye.

So near yet so far, I never saw the beauty of everything you are.

Lives being built in other worlds
Are suspended for Christmas and New Year.
A smile, a laugh in a smoke-filled room, a walk,
A sudden urge dutifully dispelled into winter chilled air.

So near yet so far, an instant connection but my life belonged elsewhere.

The realisation of life's imperfections
Offers newfound freedom to open invitations.
"Stay at mine, of course it's fine, this is my time."
Through open doors step auld acquaintance.

So near yet so far, somehow familiar but I don't know who you are.

Party time in party house,
Break the shackles that tie us down.
Somebody new is on my latest list
Of the people with whom I want to share my good times.

So near yet so far, invited to my parties because I
want to have you there.

Brave hearts defeat the trepidation,
A chance to meet at a railway station.
Awkward teenage feelings in grown up minds,
Ground-breaking moments over hurried curry.

So near yet so far, I was outside the train station
waiting for your car.

Fear of committal wanes, time to explore,
Take to the skies to find out more.
Trains and planes and wonderful places
Wash in on waves of sun-drenched windswept
kisses.

So near yet so far, travelling and exploring
something magical to share.

Saturday nights invite gastronomic delights.
Late night talks and Sunday walks make time fly.
Fleeting moments that recur with happiness
Burst into bloom at the end of each work-hard week.

So near yet so far, I love to see the beauty
of everything you are!

MANCHESTER

Let's pop over the border from Normal Town for some verses about one of our neighbouring cities...

Manchester the Magnificent

Manchester the magnificent: -

Citizens of Tesco eating alfresco
On a beautiful summer's day.
Peaceful, majestic, social, domestic,
The perfect place for work and play.
No one here worried when developers hurried
To create des-res from decay,
Nobody wept as the city fathers swept
The dirty old town away.

A million miles away, just down the road: -

Under the carpet the true city still throbs,
No room here for new money snobs,
Just the craggy skinned hard-faced yobs,
The ones with no future, no homes and no jobs.

Welcome to Manchester: -

The airport billboards proudly proclaim,
As people move from arrivals to taxis and trains.
"Is this the right place dad?" The kids start to complain
As they step from the terminal into the rain.

In the ring of the disenfranchised: -

The promises of a bright tomorrow
Turned out to be a fop.
The 24-hour party people

Don’t dance ‘til they drop.
The airport trains pass through
And the taxis never stop.
The city-break weekend tourists
Don’t come here to shop.

All praise the new suburbia: -

Where death is so common
The bereaved no longer grieve.
Where instinctively the people
Here learn to bob and weave.
Yet still the talented dare to dream
And somehow still believe
That if they try hard and get lucky,
One day they can leave...

And go to magnificent Manchester: -

The place where ultimate greed
Replaced philanthropy.
Where windswept and interesting
Is regarded as insanitary.
Where free and radical thinking
is treated as insanity.
Where there’s loads of hard cash
but little room for humanity.

The *Undustrial* Revolution happened here.

Climbing into tomorrow – falling into yesterday.

Sitting Under a Manchester Sky

Sitting under a Manchester sky,
Watching as the city goes by.
Shades of grey reflect in their eyes
As the passers-by get on with their lives.

I'm going to sit here in this place
Until I can pick out your pretty face.
Waiting for the heat to come,
A fleeting moment in the sun.
A flightless bird soaring high.
Up into the urban sky.

Lying under a Manchester moon.
Hoping that the morning don't come too soon.
Come tomorrow you'll be gone,
Back to the place where you belong.

I don't want to lie here in the cold,
Feeling young inside but growing old.
Waiting for the heat to come,
A fleeting moment in the sun.
A flightless bird soaring high.
Up into the urban sky.

Standing under a Manchester sun,
Can't believe I'm having so much fun
Trying out things that I've never done.
In the place where I was born.

I’m going to stand here as long as I can.
Hold your hand and become a man.
Finally the heat has come,
Golden moments in the sun.
Big strong wings that make me fly.
Up and beyond this urban sky.

Take me to the city of your kindness,
Give me eyes to see through all this blindness.
There is no misery in the simplicity of the childish,
Just mischief and laughter and the fun of being foolish.

Walking in the Manchester rain,
Listening to the voices in my brain.
The drizzle tells me that I’m not insane
And that one day we’ll be holding hands again.

Sitting under a Manchester sky.

A Manchester Mocking Bird

The day that Harper Lee came to Harpurhey
She got this idea that just wouldn't go away.
It started with a conversation that she overheard
When a pub landlord said:
"Bob! You'd better have a word!"

It all came about because a local lass with a foul mouth and sarcastic lip
Was upsetting all the regulars by giving them some jip.
"Have a word, Bob! She's disturbing the ambience
And if she carries on like that, she'll be leaving in an ambulance...
Or worse...a hearse!"

As Harper Lee sat at the bar sipping her brandy and Coke
The atmosphere became more intense with every quip and every joke.
Harper Lee jotted down notes as a local lag subtly inferred
That if the fun-poker didn't shut up and sling her hook
He was going to kill that mocking bird!

Bob duly carried out his order and asked her to leave real quick.
The woman was somewhat surprised and enquired:
"What's up can't they take a bit of stick?"
"They usually can" said Bob "but not on darts night."
"Oh God I didn't realise!" said the woman as she took flight.

Her exit was greeted with sighs of relief as peace was restored once more,
An embarrassed looking mocking girl scuttled out of the door.

Harper Lee left the pub and left England the very next day,
She headed off to a small town somewhere in the USA.
When she perused her notes from her travels, she'd picked up something vital,
She was going to write a novel one day and now at last she had a title!

The Ardwick on the Green

A multitude assembled one morning in Ardwick
To stare mesmerised at something truly fantastic.
There was something lurking on the green,
The strangest creature that they had ever seen.
It had great big ears and a skinny snakelike tongue
That protruded from a snout that was extraordinarily long.
It was digging up the grass with trowel like claws
Then licking up insects into porcine jaws.

An expert arrived from Belle-Vue Zoo on a bus
To inspect the weird mammal that was causing such a fuss.
He studied and pondered for what seemed like ages
Then concluded it had not escaped from any of his cages.
"What is it then?" asked a gentleman from the council.
"Not sure!" said the zoologist as he took out his pencil.
He sketched the strange critter from every aspect and view,
Before announcing "It's a great discovery, something unique and new!"

A senior curator from London's Museum of Natural History
Turned up next, bemused. This creature was a mystery!
"We need to name this animal and photograph it at every angle.

It needs to be categorised and catalogued as
something completely original."
He continued "I think I'm going to call it a
Porkamadirrel
Because it looks like a cross between a Pig, an
Armadillo and a Squirrel."

This offended the man from the council and his
intervention was quick:
"We should name it after where it was discovered.
Let's call it an Ardwick!"

'Hurrah!'

The name was agreed and all the details were written
down.
So you would expect there to be an animal named after
this part of town.
Unfortunately, the curator's handwriting was poor and
his pencil was not very sharp,
So the creature that should have been an Ardwick
ended up being known as an Aardvark!

SHOPPING

Time to go shopping on the superhighway and the high street...

Squatty Potty

Have you ever heard of the Squatty Potty?
It's a device to raise your knees above your botty.
It may seem absurd but I have heard
That it helps to produce the perfect turd.

Search it on the Internet
And within a moment I'll bet,
That you'll be thinking:
'Why haven't I got one yet?'

Order one quick it will make your toileting slick,
Just a few clicks of the mouse
Can bring a Squatty Potty to your house
And for just a few quid you'll be glad that you did.

Because with a little Squatty Potty training
You'll find that you'll no longer be straining.
It's the perfect solution to your morning constitutional,
What a wonderful contribution to your daily ablutions.

It's a virtual revolution that is very exciting,
Solving the problem we all apparently have
With the way we are shiteing.

It will help to right the unstated wrong
Of our outdated position for creating a pong,
A new 21st century you,
A new millennial way to poo,
At least that's what it said in the online review.

Laxatives and Buscopan are the medicines of fools,
Squatty Potty is the simple way
To well formed, happy stools.

Get a new perspective on life,
Or at least a part of it.
Untangle the way that you sit,
Change the angle at which you shit.

Supermarket Slag

They say:
"Do you want a loyalty card?
You can earn reward points on your shopping to spend when times get hard."

The question keeps being asked by corporate email
or by staff
and it causes me to consider,
then it causes me to laugh.
Because when I look at my varied collection of plastic carrier bags,
I realise what I've become, I'm a supermarket slag.

I can't commit my spending habits to a single entity,
it would belie my sense of freedom
to give in to a shopping identity.
A meandering wonderer,
a wandering shop to shop philanderer,
who ponders in the moment and thinks upon the spot,
considering what takes my fancy,
what do I need? What have I already got?
Constantly spotting bargains and yellow label teasers
to buy for another day
then store in the 'whoopsie' freezer.

When it comes to buying supplies for now
or the stuff I might want later,
it's an unashamed admission
that loyalty is not in my nature.

I don’t shop to win bonus points
in a store where the prices are higher,
I can’t commit my budget to a single source supplier.

Luxury or staple? Best before or use by?
Decisions to be made!
Do I fulfil my requirement for necessity
or my other desire for greed?

Of all the checkouts in all the world
I had to walk into here,
and the question’s always the same
whether from machine or human cashier.
“Have you got our loyalty card?”
they always enquire and I say “No! No way!”

I don’t want to give your corporation
all my shopping data,
I’ll pay for my goods, be on my way
and I might see you later,
because I’m the guy in Lidl
with a battered Waitrose bag,
An exemplary, bona fide supermarket slag!

TRAVEL

Everybody needs a break sometimes so let's leave the confines of Normal Town and explore...

Kindred Spirit

I've discovered a small town near an old canal basin.
It’s an underrated place that is quietly amazing.
It's not a location on many a tourist bucket list
But it holds a gentle attraction that is hard to resist.

A place where many of the inhabitants are slightly quirky,
Where the vessels are usually long and the waters often murky.
People live contented in a self-created micro-society,
In a valley formed by rivers and geological activity.

The river was tamed by industrial requirements,
The navigation is testament to human achievements.
Excavated by hard labour and brutal determination,
A living nightmare helped realise dreams of mass transportation.

This is the place where my journey starts and ends,
Timeless and tiring via old passages and old friends,
On routes created by the hard toil of a short-lived era,
Moving slowly, flat bottomed, into a Yorkshire Riviera.

Cruising slowly forward, no specific goals in mind,
Away from the worries, no hurry here, just downtime.
Dreaming, with my girl in a hidden world of tranquillity
Where the industry of the past collides with natural beauty.

Sharing the journey with ducks and swans and heron,
Trees and bridges mirrored in the sunlit waters we delight in.
Wildflowers and dragonflies provide a visual
accompaniment
To the diesel engine as it chugs a rhythm of mild
contentment.

Exploring familiar places from a different perspective.
Feeling at peace with a mind that is calm and
reflective.
Sleeping and eating on industrial steps at nature's
door.
The serene scene becomes addictive, give me more!

Towpath brief acquaintances pass and
wave and smile.
Gentle joy unfolds in ripples, mile after mile.
A joy that disparate people are drawn to and inherit,
Stood on the stern with a steady hand
on the tiller of our Kindred Spirit.

Dirty Old Tour

Forget the Yellow Brick Road.
Don't bother with paths of gold.
You don't need an open top bus
To travel with us.
Turn your eyes towards the floor
And follow the trail of manure
On the shite-seeing tour.

Our guide will tell tales like you never heard,
As you follow him through the stream of turds.
He'll provide a raincoat and a waterproof map
As you walk in single file through the crap.
You'll find a new way to enjoy the obscure
As you follow the trail of manure
On the shite-seeing tour.

Just direct your wet tourist feet
To the shitty side of the street.
Look up and see something wonderful and pretty,
Enjoy the culture of our amazing city,
Before you look down once more
As you follow the trail of manure
On the shite-seeing tour.

Roll up, turn up, come on down
Share in the joy of this dirty old town.
Come and have a majestic mucky time,
Follow us through the digested slime.
It's cool and smelly and slightly impure,
As you follow the trail of manure
On the shite-seeing tour.

Come with us and feel alive,
Trip Advisor scores us five out of five.
Our faecal delights will never offend,
What a perfect addition to a dirty weekend.
It's probably unique,
Something you've never done before
As you follow the trail of manure
On the shite-seeing tour.

Never Netherlands

I'm off to the Netherlands
Where the land lies flat and low.
A place where the pace may be perceived
As being a little slow
But in reality, it's pretty quick,
Without ever being manic.
Things just seem to get done,
Without the need for panic.

And of course, everything is flat,
Well there's nothing wrong with that!
Hills are not necessarily required
To make a person feel inspired.

A closer horizon creates a different perspective,
One where inspiration can be found in the introspective,
When there is a lack of distant landscapes,
It's much easier to focus on the nearer shapes.

Proximity comes to the fore.
Without the eye being distracted by a need to explore.
Suddenly the artistic value of a far-off distant land
Is far less interesting than something close at hand.

Faces, flowers, buildings and patterns dominate
Artistic heritage expressed in townscapes and portraits,
A land reclaimed from the sea with few border nations,
Yet a country at the heart of Europe,
With all its complications.

A land of history, order, logic,
Progression, art and commerce,
Where sex, drugs and public services,
Are not seen as perverse.
An eco-friendly landscape of canals,
Of symmetry and dykes,
Perfect for exploring on boats and trains and bikes.

It all sounds wonderful in the Netherlands,
It sounds like a never-never land.
Why can't we all be like that?
Well maybe we could be if the world was flat.

But travel and discovery prove that it's not,
So we have to adapt to the landscapes that we've got,
With mountains and valleys that cannot be ignored,

Can I live the Dutch life forever?

Of course not, I'd get bored!

Thoughts of Saltburn-by-the-Sea

Footfalls on firm wet sand as we walk hand in hand
where the land meets the sea.
Laurence's figures form like apparitions then
disintegrate
Onto the damp canvas of the mist laden air.
The moist sea fret wraps the landscape in a heavy
net curtain,
Hiding the distant saline horizon and blurring the
opposing hills into an opaque perspective.
Grey shades dominate the spectrum.
Yet revealed realms of subtle blues, and green hues
colour the foam of breaking waves.
Beige flatness lined with black fights back against
the shrouded sunlight,
So dim, but still able to create reflections on the thin
sheen of saturated sands.
Listen!
To the cries of ghostly gulls as they swoop and glide
out of foggy skies,
To the voices in the shadows, the barks of invisible
dogs and of course,
To the relentless white noise of the sea as wave
upon wave crashes through the mist
Onto the beach with a constant rhythm,
Creating a singular beautiful harmony of pleasure
and contentment.
Somewhere, inspired, in the murky mystery,
Laurence picks up his brush.

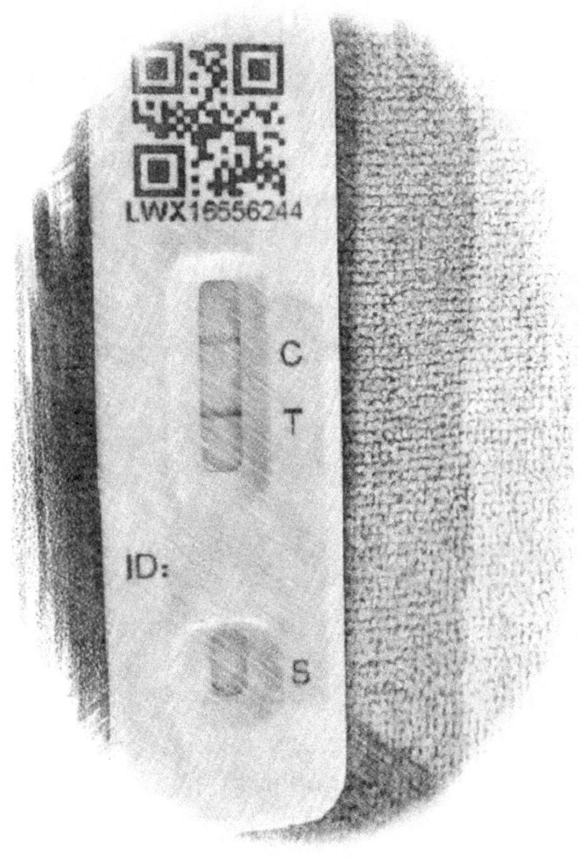
LWX16556244
C
T
ID:
S

COVID-19

The whole world including Normal Town was affected by the pandemic which spread during 2020...

Unfinished Chapter

Pneumonia, pandemic, pandemonium and panic.
What is this thing that is happening on my planet?
News crews telling bad news with sugar coated faces,
Stuttered internet interviews with experts in strange places.
Switch it off, make it go away, I've had enough bad news for today.

Curled up on the couch hiding, like the author who can't finish his next chapter
To enrapture his readers and capture the audience he requires,
The very thing to which he aspires;
Seems a place of safety, a place of maybe,
A place for "Hey day just go away to where my heyday went."

Time spent in coiled up lament for an exquisitely billed non-event
That was going to rock the world, but the world turned its back.
The venues are empty!

In our world of plenty the people are elementary to its very existence.
They are the force for constitution, the force for resistance,
The guests at the feast.

The stupid and the wise without whom society is like a bread with no yeast and it fails to rise.
Normal Town becomes abnormal, human interaction becomes informal
As I pass by with a suspicious glance, I might nod a greeting if you keep your distance.

Feedback can be nice, or it can slice your heart in two,
When you share your soul with the world, the world will judge what you do.
Would I swap my lonely kitchen theatre for a night at the Palladium?
Do I crave a sell-out concert at my own sweet empty stadium?
Do I want to play online? Well, it helps to pass the time, that just messes with my mind.

I want to return to the human race, I long to hug and kiss a warm sweet face.

My gratitude and admiration goes to those trying to reinstate the broken pieces,
Trying to stop the runaway train, heroes dying as they are thrown into flames
That burn our flawed system of existence to the ground.

Sacrificial lambs with burns on healing hands,
The hands of love that are trained to mend.
I'm in awe but like them, like all of us, like the author,
I want this unfinished chapter to end.

The Spring That Never Was

The market squares and the shopping malls were empty, nobody was there,
There was something odd and eerie not just here but everywhere.
What seemed like a nothing at first, just an over-hyped insignificance
At which we'd laughed and joked about, began to make a difference.
A difference to our friends, our families, our way of life, our jobs
Crept then swept into the global society in the spring that never was.

The trees bore their blossom as our humour turned to grief and disbelief,
The daffodils grew and the flowers bloomed and the blossom gave way to leaf.
The sunshine came and the birds returned to nest and sing in newly green trees
Whilst the human race seemed to stop in shock in a dystopian make-believe.
A make-believe world of confinement, locked pub doors and closed down shops,
A world where the internet ignited like a wildfire in the spring that never was.

For a while divided political loyalties were replaced by coherent coalition
As the capitalist bubble burst and was replaced by a new type of socialism.

At first supermarket shelves were emptied in frenzy as people stocked up on their rations
But slowly in the enormity of the situation, greed gave way to compassion.
People began to care and support each other as they clapped and rattled pans and pots.
They rang, messaged and video chatted, caught up in the spring that never was.

As the birds reclaimed the empty sky whilst corporations urged a rapid solution,
Mother Nature breathed a fresh sigh of relief, for once without any pollution.
Fresh air, fresh minds that fuelled by time found new ways to express their creations,
Will soon give way to be consumed once more by real life's hectic frustrations.
When the world returns to the new normal and we assess the loss and count the cost,
I hope that we remember what was learnt and what we have gained in the spring that never was.

Ten Days in Autumn

Ten days in autumn and a massive threat to the
freedom of UK citizens rose again.
And it showed how it is relentless and remorseless
as it began to inflict more pain.
Some may assume that it was the Covid-19 virus,
but that's not what I meant,
I meant the brutal gang of elitist bullies at the heart
of the British government.
As they created confusion and division in the hour of
our greatest need
By slowly withdrawing support and consensus in the
pursuit of their own greed.
An insatiable greed for money and power and
maintaining an unfair status quo.
A greed that thinks that it knows best,
better than the people in the know.

Hypocrisy, lies, and smokescreens, cunningly
backed up by indecision
Bring misery to those invited to the kangaroo court,
then treated with derision.
They honed their skills cocooned in public schools
indoctrinated whilst shielded from reality.
They perfected 'smile as you kill', kind public words,
to disguise their closed-door brutality.
They are open to negotiation and prepared to talk
through options when opinions are divided
And of course, they will listen to what we have to say
before doing what they've already decided.

The lions from the north rose from slumber taking
people's concerns believing they had choices
Only to be played like a fiddle in the chambers of
horror, naïve, betrayed, silenced voices.

During ten days in autumn, devolution, that great
solution, was muted by those in command,
Political laryngitis burned its throat as The Great
Northern Powerhouse was smashed to the ground.
The request for true fairness, the hopes of the people
washed away with the tears of their mayor,
As true colour returned to a sick face at number ten.
Ten days in autumn, three tiers of despair.

The 2020 Blues

Santa's having a day off this year,
He can't be arsed with Christmas cheer,
He can't get his sleigh and reindeer into gear.
He's got the 2020 blues.

His beard is unkempt and his belly's fat and soft.
He's left his decorations up in the loft.
He says, "I think I'll just have to take some time off."
He's got the 2020 blues.

He's furloughed his elves,
They don't know when they'll be back
There's no-one at the factory to fill Santa's sack.
Santa can't afford the overheads; he's had to cut back.
He's got the 2020 blues.

It's out of control and he's not to blame,
Unprecedented circumstances
Have made the world insane.
He says he thought about trying
But it just wouldn't be the same.
He's got the 2020 blues.

It's not practical
To get his work done in a single night,
When he'd need to quarantine at every border
for a fortnight
And breaking lock-down rules
To check his eyesight just wouldn't be right,
He's got the 2020 blues.

He's made a list and he's checked it more than twice,
But this year tradition
Is something we'll have to sacrifice.
Santa knows that Christmas without him
Just won't be as nice,
But he's got the 2020 blues.

So Santa's having a day off this time.
This year he recommends that
We buy all our presents on-line.
And he sends his best wishes and
Hopes next year will be fine,
But for now,
He's got the 2020 blues.

LONELINESS

There are so many wonderful people in Normal Town but when the front door closes anybody can succumb to loneliness, depression or anxiety ...

Pyromaniac

The lone man makes a fire and considers his solitude
for a while.

But as rockets fly and flames grow higher, he breaks
into a smile.

This is no time for loneliness, this is a time to burn our
fears.

Time to forge a new bright future as every flame
appears

And dances in the face of the dark autumn night and
sheds light,

As it glows and shows its random patterns, prancing,
shimmering delight.

Then falls and fades and flickers until the man looks for
something more to burn

And he feeds the fire damp wood, which seems no
good, hoping that brightness will return.

For a moment the cold and dark creep back as the
golden flames refrain,

Until the latent heat makes the moisture retreat and
it's time to dance again!

One Horse Race

Some things don't work out as planned
And life seems to have dealt a dreadful hand,
I thought I was on a winner I just can't understand
How I ended up alone in this desolate place.
I bet on a loser in a one-horse race.

It's not best policy to sit around and mope,
It's not a situation without any hope.
It's a time to keep tugging, not drop the rope.
The experience of failure is not a disgrace,
When you've bet on a loser in a one-horse race.

The cockney on the telly keeps telling me to bet.
My bookmaker's account isn't getting closed down yet.
If I do it responsibly, who knows what I'll get?
I'll study the odds, the conditions and the pace,
Then bet on a loser in a one-horse race.

Things aren't always as bad as they seem.
What could have been a nightmare was only a dream
And the risk that I took wasn't too extreme.
I only lost fifty pence in this particular case.
When I bet on a loser in a one-horse race.

The Calm Panic

It should be oh so easy, just a normal weekend morning
When a sudden fear takes hold,
Without any reason or warning.
And your heart feels like the flutter
Of a wounded bird attempting flight,
A constant disjointed effort with an overtone of fright.

Thoughts of others, tasks unfinished,
Consume a confused mind.
Seek out the refuge of somnolence
To leave those thoughts behind.

Fall into more confusion, wandering vivid dreamscapes,
Waking, dozing, jumping,
A fluttering bird with no escape.

Waking, shaking nightmare,
Twitching madness, phobias abound,
As the brutal fist of a subtle intruder
Softly beats you to the ground.

Fear of silence, fear of people, fear of being alone.
Debilitation, palpitations, frustration at the panic station.

Fear of something. Fear of the unknown.

Living in the calm before the storm.

POLITICS

Normal Town goes to the polls, so whilst it may not be wise to talk about politics, sometimes it is inevitable ...

Election Day

It's polling day come and have your say.
It's your right of constitution
Your only contribution
To democracy.

Mark your cross in the box of your candidate,
Give someone the mandate to represent you.
No matter what your views
It's something you should do.
It's your democratic right
To give your assistance
Or show your resistance and who knows?
It just might not be pointless.
It might make a difference
To something somewhere despite your doubt,
You can influence the issues
That you really care about.

It's just a short trip to the polling station,
It's your only valid comment
On the state of the nation.
Honour and respect our ancestors of note,
Who fought and protested for your right to vote.
They were passionate and determined
That the population
Should be heard not undermined,
And that we all have a voice,
An undeniable choice,
The rich the poor, the strong the weak,
A silent confidential, opportunity to speak.

Get out and vote. It might not go your way
But at least you'll know that you had your say.
Get out and vote, if you don't it will be a shame,
And when it all turns to shit,
You'll only have yourself to blame.

VOTE, VOTE, VOTE

And if your hopes are all denied,
At least you can console yourself
With the knowledge that you tried.

Send in the Clown

Ill equipped to lead but oh so quick to quip,
an impressive speed of tongue and a convincing wit
that gives lip service to the detail
of serious situations,
camouflaged by skilfully crafted verbal
perambulations.

Wonderful, wicked, a witty wag,
a charismatic suitor,
laughing and wisecracking his way
into an uncertain future.
An intentionally accidental, disorderly façade,
bumbling and fumbling, tumble-tousle-haired.

Playful rhetoric littered with historical reference
distort and distract from an unstructured
selfish ambivalence.
The pied piper playing tunes to the politically
neglected,
Jack the lad, the joker in the pack, who somehow
became respected.

An incredible illusion, a majestic sleight of hand,
tricks of such confusion, no one could understand.
From a hatful of white doves, blindfolded rabbits
appear.

“Be brave my chums, the answer’s here,
the answer ***is*** clear!”

Tough times need tough measures and we’re
all in this together.
No admission of the demolition, only a promise to
build back better!

Levelling up after dragging us down,
the elitist circus rolled into town,
Whilst Shelley’s fabled lions remain in slumber,
send in the clown!

BACK TO NORMAL TOWN

Let's head back to Normal Town for some contemplation, observation and celebration ...

Something is Missing

There are very few photographs of true happiness,
Because when truly happy we don't have time.
We may get some snaps of before or after
But they're just the scene of the crime.

There are very few photographs of true sadness,
It's not something we want to record.
We don't feel it appropriate to photograph moments
When misery has us absorbed.

There are plenty of photographs of the other times,
When we feel the inclination,
So our pictorial, historical footprint
Is a source of misinformation.

The same is true of writing,
Most stories and biographies are reflective laments,
Where we use our notes, memories and equipment.
To try to recall the reality of events.

I could make an argument for art,
But the process takes quite a while,
And whilst the final creation may be the subject,
It is represented by the artist's style.

Surely journalists, news and documentaries?
Yes, they capture real-time events for us to share,
But as observers behind lenses, computers and pens,
Shielded from the actual passion, thrills and despair.

So the biography of all humanity
And its substantial, extraordinary endeavour
Is incomplete as parts exist only in minds,
Which will one day be lost forever.

Shoe Rack

My shoe rack is full of orthotic devices.

Which aim to stop the pain from my
degenerating frame.
There is one for my back so that the next time it
cracks or spasms in a sciatic attack,
I can wear it around the house
to brace my troubled vertebrae as it delivers
mild electric shocks
designed to stimulate my spine and make
everything feel fine...

For a while!

Two other appliances catch my eye.
They support my thighs on the rare occasions
when I exercise.
They keep my muscles firm and tight,
otherwise
my Vastus or Sartorius just might
rupture or rip
as I extend my leg in an attempt
to block or kick.

I can see my obligatory tubi-grips,
that squeeze my knees
or squash my calves which have
an inclination to strain
or cramp devoid of reason or warning.
I combine them with a warming spray

that can burn and sting the eyes
or other tender places
if it gets onto my hands during application.

Then lower down, closer to the ground,
my ankle straps.
Joints that need support
before attempting any sport
or they will roll and bend
into awkward positions in which, they were never
intended to be.
The result of which
is weeks of limping immobility ...

I don't like that at all!

So in the corner of my hall is a frame
Designed to store footwear
of all shapes and sizes,
Now repurposed and utilised
for items to cope
With strains and sprains
and plantar fasciitis...

My shoe rack is full of orthotic devices.

Waiting Room Blues

What's to do in a waiting room?
It's a difficult conundrum.
Seven hours at the A & E
Certainly lacks some fun.
What's to do in a waiting room?
It's not easy to explain.
In this boring place with empty faces
Waiting for someone to call out their name.

What's to do in a waiting room?
I can fiddle with my phone.
Then curse and drat when the battery goes flat
And wonder what time I'll get home.
What's to do in a waiting room?
I can watch the patient info screen
As it scrolls on repeat slide after slide,
Full of stuff that I've already seen.

What's to do in the waiting room?
I can watch the clock go tick.
Then notice that it is three minutes fast
And wonder why nobody fixed it.
What's to do in the waiting room?
Three minutes into the future.
They call out for somebody else,
Oh well, I'll have to wait some more.

What's to do in the waiting room?
I can strike up a conversation
With a stranger, where our only congruence
Is the cause of our frustration.
What's to do in a waiting room?
I can listen to an old lady complain.
That she saw a triage nurse two hours ago
And now she's here, waiting again.

What's to do in a waiting room?
The car park will cost me a shedload.
As more time goes by, further charges apply,
God, I wish I'd parked up the road.
What's to do in a waiting room?
I can wonder about the NHS,
Is that great institution, our world leading system,
Now just an underfunded mess?

What's to do in a waiting room?
I can reflect upon my malady.
Maybe it's not such an indisposition
And can be treated another day?
What's to do in a waiting room?
The clue is in the name.
It's a sure-fire way to squander some time
In a wasted waiting game.

Christmas Wishes

Imagine a city where nothing beautiful exists...
Smash a bottle on the floor and create a garden...
Smell the flowers.

Go to a busy place, see the words floating in the roof space ...
Catch them in a butterfly net and take them home on the bus.

Let words dance on the pages of your imagination...
Close your eyes as you read them out loud.

Walk in a place of memories until your legs ache...
Rest by some water until it joins with the sky.

Think of a time of happiness...
Dissolve it in water then drink it.

Search the sky for gentle waves...
Float or swim in the sounds they make.

Breathe in the air of a silent place...
Fill it with music as you breathe out.

Make a sequence with your mind...
Play it over and over until your mind is complete.

Open up the fragility of your heart...
Take the contents to a place of beauty.

Plant something you like...
Watch it grow to manage.

Starry Starry Night

"Don't shoot! Don't shoot!"
A thunderbolt leaves his boot
And breaks the nervous tension of the night
To disbelieving, all relieving, glorious delight.

Beads of sweat glisten like a jewelled crown on the brow of the hero king
As he walks the grounds of his palatial home where his loyal citizens bow and sing.
His eyes of passion swell and proud teardrops roll briefly down his cheeks
As he strolls around and greets every friend and foe that he meets
Some delirious in victory others gracious in defeat.
They embrace him as they stand at the feet of a giant,
A humble hero who fights to the end and remains defiant.

Not long ago our hero's muscles that once rippled
Were savaged and ravaged and crippled.
The citizens began to doubt his resilience
But he fought back and returned to the brilliance
As the leader of a band of brothers whose individual talents are the fabric of dreams,
Sewn together by the dream weaver the maker of teams; and even he it seems
Realises the importance of a strong thread,

A reliable and solid head
And a heart that is true,
A heart that will be forever blue.

Even the dream weaver shouts “Don't shoot!”
But the king doesn't listen
He follows his heart, he believes in his mission
To make our dreams come true
To lead this team, his team

Out of the blue.

“Don't shoot! Don't shoot!”
A thunderbolt leaves his boot
And breaks the nervous tension of the night
To disbelieving, all relieving, glorious delight.

Raise A Glass

Throw up the bunting, raise the flag, and start dancing in the street.
Let's get this party started, get our community back on its feet.
Crack out the bottles, pop the corks, share out the wines and beers,
Celebrate our Queen Elizabeth who's been at it for 70 years.

From post war austerity to now she's been the figurehead of a monarchy,
Impotent and powerless in the face of our pseudo-democracy.
Muted opinions, publicly silent on personally held views,
Unable to comment on the politics that fills our daily news.

Yet somehow, duty bound, she projects her personality
On her subjects, whom for many, she defines their nationality.
Like a majestic swan on the Thames, gliding, guiding, dignified
Above the silted secret underworld that the murky waters hide.

Handed a job for life, without application, by an accident of fate.

A dubious hereditary tradition made her an unelected head of state.
When the 70s punks sang God Save the Queen at the silver jubilee,
It was with a massive dose of tongue in cheek and a pinch of irony.
It's now 45 years later on and that song is not forgotten
But the ageing singer has mellowed and might not be so rotten.

He, like me, can disagree with the ancestral right to be queen or king
But beneath the crown we can see and respect an individual human being
With a personality of caring and love and a diplomatic air,
Scarred by personal tragedies and sorrow...
but still there.

A familiar constant year after year in a changing world of variables
An eloquent well-travelled ambassador, hardworking and reliable.
She's lived her life in the relentless service of her country since 1952,
So I'll raise a glass to the grand old lass, respect and credit where credit is due.

AGE AND MORTALITY

Age and mortality are unavoidable realities that we often avoid thinking about, but they need to be faced, even in Normal Town...

Double Life

Everybody lives twice,
But only parents really get to know it.
When they reach an age when their kids are all grown up
Into men or women or something else maybe?

And the person stood before you that was once your little baby,
A developing child with inquisitive mind, innocently immature,
Is now a fully-fledged complex lifeform that isn't dependent on you anymore.

They loved you, they hated you and they took your precious time,
But you gave it unconditionally, then later argued every line
To try to make them understand this world the same as you do
But they challenged and contradicted before they ultimately exposed you.

No longer in control you begin to learn about something different
From the perspective of a new breed, nurtured by you but free and divergent.

Memories!

Recall and remember the child and seek the innocence,
Of the person standing in front of you who now bears no resemblance
To that unformed version of what they used to be.

They grow and they move away, they live again!
They change until only the love remains.
For the life of the pupa and the emergent form,
A bridge strong enough to link and support two lives.

Everybody lives twice.

Golden Years

I feel a bit different from the other kids, mum,
I feel a bit out of sorts,
I can't understand all the mathematical stuff
And I'm not very good at sports.
The big kids keep on bullying me,
The teachers all think that I'm a fool,
I can't find anything positive here,
I wish I was back at the old school.

I don't like the homework that the teachers set,
I don't feel I'm ready to do that yet,
They're trying to make me into an all-rounder
But what if I fail, what if I flounder,
What if I miss my target in my SATs?
I'm lost in this place full of tables and stats.

I want to go back and play in the sandpit,
Make shapes and noises that don't really fit
Into this incomprehensible shit
That they call an academy.

I'm sorry mum please don't be mad at me
When I come home in tears, expressing all my fears
Because I can't stand the thought
Of this for the next five or six years.
I used to wake up in the morning
Looking forward to my day
But now I want to stay in bed and make it go away.

I'm sorry son to hear about your struggle and your strife
But I'm afraid that you'll have to face it,
It's a valuable preparation for life,
Which is full of stats and disappointments
And things that we can't understand,
But we all have to get through it whilst keeping our instinctive desire to mess about in the sand.

There is a little child inside us all
Never totally forgotten,
It's our only connection with humanity
When the rest of the world turns rotten.

The Age of Enlightenment

I have reached an age at which I feel enlightened,
All of my senses have suddenly been heightened,
My money belt may have a requirement to be
tightened.
Does it scare me? Not a bit, I'm certainly not
frightened.

My views on life don't need any reassurance,
I can be who I am without any fear or reluctance,
My kids will be fine, they know I've got insurance.
Their only problem is the one of my own endurance.

I can look at the papers and watch the news,
Read books and watch films then write
my own reviews,
I can throw away possessions that I'm never
going to use
And have influence on people so they can understand
my views.

I can give out advice and know it will be respected,
I can behave in ways that are sometimes unexpected,
I can explore the parts of me that I previously
neglected,
Because my half dead soul has now been
resurrected.

My hope for love will keep me yearning,
My thirst for knowledge will keep me learning,

My fire inside is ignited and for now it keeps on
burning,
I can hate things in the world but still it keeps on
turning.

I can dance in public without feeling self-aware,
I can talk out loud when no-one else is there,
I can cry with emotion and know it shows that I care
Or hide and avoid the things that I really cannot bear.

I can see clever people who didn't go to university,
I can appreciate the impact of all human diversity,
After all, we all have the right to our own identity
And I'm ready to feel what it's like to just be me.

I have reached an age that I thought was far away,
An age that just crept up on me and appeared
along the way,
An age that I assumed would be cold and old and grey
But it's warm and gold and beautiful and full of
newness every day.

Existential

Talking to the walking dead on memory lane.
A miserable thought followed a short burst of
nostalgia
Then soft, subtle, brutal pain.
These were the people of my formative years,
telling tales that would reduce a glass eye to tears.

Baby, baby where did our life go?
Why did it go so fast when it used to go so slow?
I hardly know you now, a stranger!
And you haven't got a clue
about the version of life that absorbed me
since I fooled around with you.
Echoes of years long gone but still so near and
dear, bring to life my lucky breaks then re-instil
my hidden fear...

Of mortality.

You seem to handle it so well but then
why wouldn't you?
You were always cavalier,

Fuck tomorrow!
Today is here!
Do it now!
Do it wow!
Fall and fail it's all OK.

Weak and frail but still today...

Somehow the same.

Live for the day!

Dance a merry dance,
for come tomorrow
we may never get the chance.
Dance until we drop,
dance until our feet fall off!

Sing and laugh and love and cry,
this is today and it's ours to enjoy...

...Existentially.

Elementary

Moriarty!

Emerges from the depths of my mind,
befuddled by busy life
I bask in the glory for a moment
as if it were a victory
to recall the name of the arch-enemy of a
fictional detective,
when in fact, it was a sign of my degenerating
memory.

Arthur Conan Doyle retreats into a corner of my
brain that for now only Google can find,
and it feels like defeat.
As I acknowledge that my knowledge
is in decline.
A deduction unworthy of 221b Baker Street.

There you sit before me. My hero, my mentor,
my hope for myself.
Now stumbling confused in murky shadows of
what I will become.
To you Sherlock Holmes is filed on an unindexed
library shelf.
You wonder why they are taking away your quiz
answers one by one.

For now, at least the people you love are still real
and familiar.
How long will they remain so despite your
determined resistance?

I feel your frustration hidden behind your kindness
and humour.
A beautiful dress is something to remember in a
present tense existence.

You fight an invisible battle as stoic and brave
as any warrior,
whilst the woman in the clothes upon which you
remark, battles at your side.
She heals your invisible wounds and gives obvious
questions an answer,
For she holds your past within her own and knows
the man inside.

And your eyes still shine with love whenever you
gaze upon her.
Recognition and appreciation of a lifetime spent
beside you.
A knowledge of whoever you are and whatever you
once were.
Holmes merges with Dick Barton, then they slowly
fade out of view.

Thank you for reading my poems. I hope that you have enjoyed them. There are some that I did not include in this collection and hopefully there are others, yet to be written, hiding on blank pages.

www.ingramcontent.com/pod-product-compliance
Lightning Source LLC
LaVergne TN
LVHW010108170826
845678LV00012B/2297

* 9 7 9 8 8 6 5 2 0 8 7 9 2 *